In Australia, there's a furry little animal that has a bill like a duck and a tail like a beaver. It has venom like a snake and lays eggs like a bird. There's a bird that lives in a hole like a mole and swims like a fish, but it can't fly. There are animals that hop on feet nearly the size of skateboards and carry their babies in their pockets. There are lizards that run on two feet like a human, and crocodiles, called salties, with teeth like a *T. rex*. Some of these animals are found nowhere else on earth. We've come more than halfway around the world to see them.

At the Top

We're here, at last, in the "land down under," so called because Australia lies below the equator in the southern hemisphere. On the way, we lost a whole day in the middle of the ocean, crossing the international dateline. And the seasons are reversed. It's fall here, and springtime at home.

Australia is so large from top to bottom that it's hot in the north and cold in the south. And, on top of *that*, when you flush the toilet, the water swirls down in the wrong direction.

Now that we're totally confused, we leave for Kakadu National Park, one of the wildest, most remote, most beautiful places anywhere. The aboriginal people of the Alligator River region have inhabited this area for more than 30,000 years. That's more than 25,000 years before the pyramids were built in Egypt. The park is 7,453 square miles, the size of Connecticut.

At the campground, we set up our tent next to the DANGER. CROCODILES. WATCH YOUR CHILDREN AND DOGS sign. We curl up in our sleeping bags, not sure what day it is, or time of year, or why crocodiles eat only children and dogs. We are resting up for our first trip to a billabong.

Yellow Water Billabong

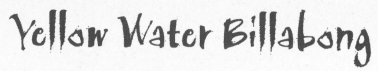

Our skiff glides out into Yellow Water Billabong, a backwater lagoon. The aboriginal word "billa" means water. The "bong" part is anybody's guess. The tiny, yellow snowflake lilies that carpet the water in the wet season give this billabong its name.

Islands of Pandanus palms, freshwater mangroves, and tall paperbark gum trees fill the landscape. Jabiru storks, five feet tall, and plumed ducks stand guard.

We search the banks for big salties, remembering not to drag our fingers in the water. Don't let the word "salty" fool you. Salties, or estuarine crocodiles, can live in the fresh water of a billabong as well as in salt water.

Fishermen pass in search of the giant barramundi, a fish that can weigh up to two hundred pounds.

A lotus bird looks as if it is walking on water. Actually it's walking on lily pads. If its chicks are threatened, the male lotus bird scoops them up under his wings and carries them to safety.

Finally, we see a big salty the same color as the bank. It's about fifteen feet long, bigger than our skiff. Its entire body rests on the bank except for its nose, which is underwater. The croc, neither moving nor breathing, has "shut down."

A crocodile can maintain a heart rate of only three to five heartbeats per minute for an hour or more.

On land, salties can run as fast as fifteen miles per hour. So, if a salty chases you, run either *sixteen* miles an hour or in a zigzag fashion. Salties can't turn fast because of their tails. *Never* run in a straight line, especially at fourteen miles per hour.

We go deeper into the paperbark swamp. The water is choked with soft, green weeds. A croc caught a thirty-pound barramundi and held on to it for two days until it rotted. Now the croc lurches half its length out of the water, shaking its head violently from side to side. SPLASH! Chunks of rotten fish go flying. We're soaked and stinking of fish.

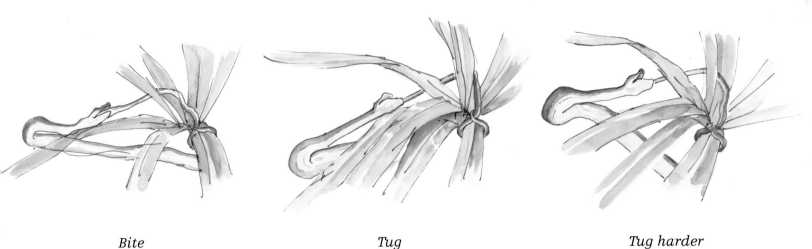

Bite   *Tug*   *Tug harder*

Time to move on. We see a strange movement in a tree. It's an olive python. Close by, a flycatcher sits calmly on its eggs. The python is swallowing another snake that is lighter in color, but the prey holds on tenaciously to the tree. We watch, spellbound. Finally, the lighter snake lets go and both snakes fall through a thick spiderweb, swinging upside down like a grotesque pendulum. The flycatcher dreamily waits for a new life to appear as another life slips away.

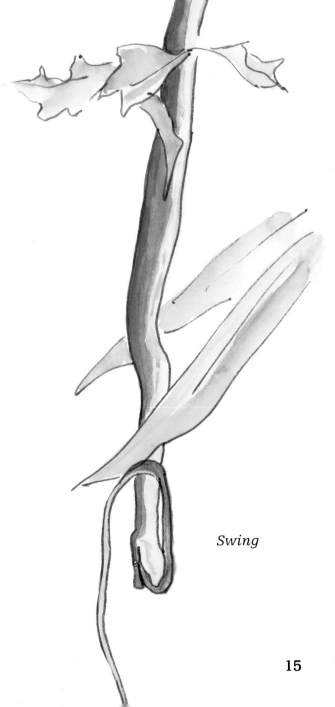

Swing

Dense stands of Pandanus line the banks on their stilt roots. Aboriginals cut the leaves into strips, roll them, and weave them into ditty bags, which they use to carry just about everything.

(ALL CIRCA 1900)

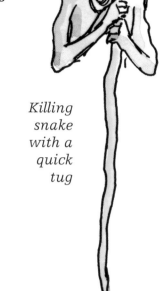

Killing snake with a quick tug

Ditty bag

On a paperbark raft

Watch out! Our skiff has drifted toward a freshwater mangrove, or "itchy" tree. If you come in contact with the grubs on the underside of the leaves, you get itchy all over.

Whoops! A big salty with enormous choppers sits so still we almost miss it. The salty is yellow-green in color, newly arrived from the ocean. The longer crocodiles are away from salt water, the darker their skins become, until they are as dark as the color of the billabong bank.

What a bonzer* croc! A big monitor lizard, called a goanna, swaggers by. Two monsters from the Jurassic era! We start the engine and leave the old fossils to themselves.

*Gathering
water-lily roots*

The landscape ahead turns to Dreamtime. The black water is framed by Pandanus and great, high stands of Arnhem bamboo. No one knows just how the bamboo got here. The aboriginals tell Dreamtime (creation) stories to explain its appearance.

As we sit quietly in this grove of Dreamtime bamboo, we think about how the aboriginal people have always lived in perfect harmony with this land.

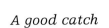

A good catch

*Boy with
young salty*

Roping a salty

The next day we leave camp in the cruiser. On either side of the road, vast yellow-brown flood plains are punctuated by blackened, newly burned stretches and bright green growth around water holes. The sky is dark gray, heavy with clouds. A dingo crosses in front of us and lies down in a fresh burn, head flat on the ground. The rest of the pack appears in the tall, green grass. Two whistling kites sit nearby on the rotting carcass of a water buffalo. Other kites circle and wheel in like vultures, trying to buzz them off. A crow joins in the confusion.

Now the dingo nearest us tugs at the buffalo with everything it's got, rips a shred of skin and meat loose, and bolts it down. For five minutes the other dingoes share the carcass.

Suddenly, a ferocious fight breaks out. The dingo near us turns, drops its hindquarters, lays back its ears, and bares its teeth in a hideous grin. The pack attacks, then gives chase when our dingo flees. No one returns to the carcass, not even the crow.

At the Bottom

Now we're flying over the "red center"—mile after mile of wild, empty, red land. We're on our way to Flinders Chase National Park on Kangaroo Island, home to almost all of Australia's wildlife *except* dingoes. Kangaroo Island is a green jewel in the cold Southern Sea, larger than the state of Rhode Island.

In 1802 it was discovered by Captain Matthew Flinders, a young British explorer. Uninhabited then, it now has a population of almost four thousand people.

In the late afternoon sun, kangaroos and Cape Barren geese graze on broad, green meadows. Flightless emus walk by, striking poses with each step, red-eyed and haughty. All are protected and unafraid of humans.

A Kangaroo Island kangaroo and the tiny joey in her pouch graze the short grass. It's as if Mama has two heads. The kangaroos on Kangaroo Island are darker, stockier, shorter limbed, and slower moving than the kangaroos on the mainland.

Hmmm.

Boink!

Yum!

Koalas hang in the tops of the rough bark manna gums like great bunches of soft, furry fruit. One tiny chocolate brown baby clings to its mother between her belly and the tree. Koala means "no drink" in the aboriginal language.

That evening, as we eat our rice laced with Tabasco sauce, four kangaroos and a brush-tailed possum invite themselves to dinner. The possum sits on our plates. Mama kangaroo intercepts our food on its way to our mouths. Another grabs our shirtfronts and rocks back onto her tail, freeing up her very strong, clawed feet—feet that could kick your guts out. She can *have* our tucker.* No worries!

Holy dooley!*

Early explorers asked the aborigines the name of the "jumping animal." They answered "kangaroo," which means "I don't understand your question."

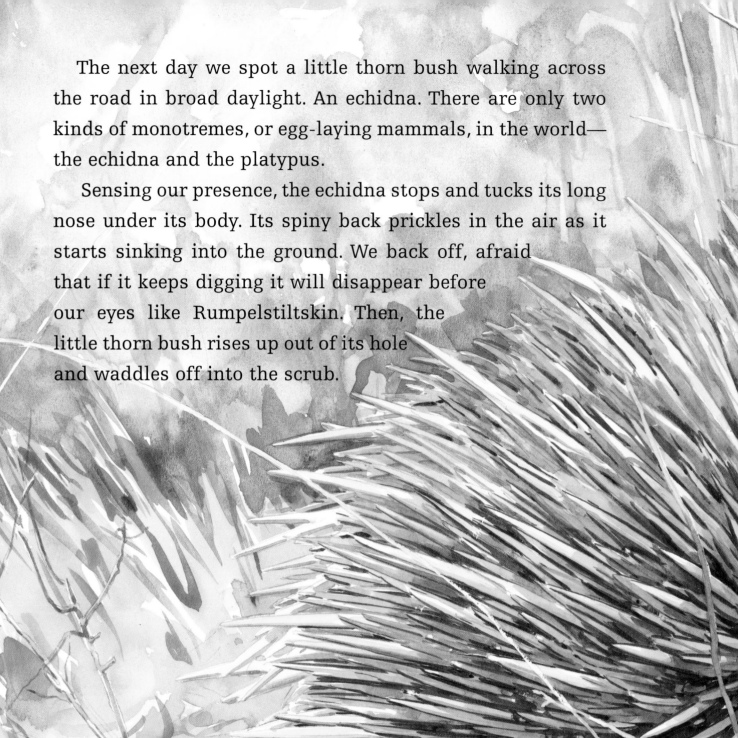

The next day we spot a little thorn bush walking across the road in broad daylight. An echidna. There are only two kinds of monotremes, or egg-laying mammals, in the world—the echidna and the platypus.

Sensing our presence, the echidna stops and tucks its long nose under its body. Its spiny back prickles in the air as it starts sinking into the ground. We back off, afraid that if it keeps digging it will disappear before our eyes like Rumpelstiltskin. Then, the little thorn bush rises up out of its hole and waddles off into the scrub.

Rocky River is a swift-moving stream full of great gum tree trunks and long, fanlike waterweeds. Moss grows everywhere. It is home to the other egg layer, the platypus.

In the pouring rain we watch the surface for the rush of bubbles that will signal its arrival. Then we realize that water striders send false platypus signals. So do leaves. And raindrops. Finally, at dusk, not five feet from us, a sleek little beaver body and soft leather bill pops to the surface.

When its nictitating membranes are shut, its eyes look like yellow headlights. When its membranes are open, we see little black shiny eyes.

PLOP! The platypus works its way underwater. Perhaps it is probing and nuzzling with its sensitive bill, feeding on insects, grubs, and small fish, storing them in its cheek pouches. It slides up into its burrow and is gone.

What luck! Seeing *both* monotremes in *one* day!

Venomous spur

Webbed foot

Not far down the coast from our campsite, there's an enchanted place called Seal Bay. The beach and surrounding dunes are littered with Australian sea lions sleeping on blankets of black seaweed, silver gulls in attendance.

We walk out on the beach, expecting all the sea lions to flee. Instead, they continue to sleep, scratch, and yawn—wonderful, whiskered creatures smelling of fish and the sea.

A big female galumphs toward us, mouth wide open. Is she greeting us or charging us? She nuzzles, bites, pushes, and barks at every other sea lion on the beach. They look at her wearily, yawn, and lie back as she waddles into the sea.

We lie down on the warm sand in the midst of the herd.
Five hundred strong, the sea lions are about ten percent of all
their kind that are left in the world. Huge bulls sit as solid as
pyramids, noses pointed to the sky, eyes closed, dozing. Two
young bulls joust on a field of seaweed. They shoulder, push,
and bite each other like puppies. When they tire of
the game, they, too, doze off. All this yawning
and sleeping is catching. Before long,
we are fast asleep too.

It is dark, very cold, and windy where the fairy penguins live. We pick our way carefully down the jumbled, slippery, lichen-covered rocks to the shore. The sun sets, and the rocks take on monstrous shapes—sea serpents, gigantic toads, and lizards.

Over the sound of the sea breaking on the rocks, we hear yapping and laughing. A crowd of fairy penguins, like little "people" dressed to the nines, waddle out of the sea after a long day of fishing.

It is our last night in this wondrous land. As we nestle into our sleeping bags, we think about the long trip home.

Fall will change back to spring. We will pick up the day we lost in the middle of the ocean, and toilets will flush in the right direction. And now we dream about those little "people" out there in that cold, black sea, laughing their hearts out.

Mates, These Are Fair Dinkum* Facts!

Australian sea lion: It swims with its front flippers and steers with its back flippers. Adult females weigh over 300 pounds. Males weigh over 800 pounds.

Barramundi: "Barramundi" is the aboriginal word for large, scaled fish. There are no young female

barramundi. All are males for the first seven years. Then they turn into females.

Echidna: (Pronounced e-kid'-na). Echidnas have two types of hair: one type for warmth; the other, with long, sharp spikes, for protection. The echidna's nose is sensitive to electrical signals from its prey. The prey is gathered on its long, sticky tongue. A baby echidna, or puggle, suckles inside its mother's pouch. When it develops spines, it is evicted.

Estuarine crocodile: It grows one foot every year for the first seven to ten years, then about an inch a year. A throat flap helps crocodiles to swallow underwater without drowning. The temperature at which crocodile eggs are kept determines the sex of the brood. Warmer temperatures produce all females.

Fairy penguin: At two pounds in weight and ten inches in height, it is the smallest penguin in the world. It can live eighteen to twenty years.

Kangaroo: Males are called boomers, females are flyers, and babies are joeys. Kangaroos travel in groups known as mobs. They are one inch long at birth and never stop growing during their lifetime. They are marsupials, which means that they carry their babies in their pouches.

Koala: Koalas live alone or in pairs, and sometimes in small groups. Males have harems of females. Koalas eat only eucalyptus leaves and shoots, and soil to aid in digestion.

Platypus: A platypus can eat its own body weight in one night. Platypus babies, also called puggles, feed on milk that oozes from pores in the mother's skin. The spurs of the male can deliver enough venom to kill a dog or make a human miserable.

Water buffalo: Introduced into Australia from Southeast Asia, feral buffalo are very destructive to the environment.